The IEA Health and Welfare Unit

Choice in Welfare Series No. 5

Morality, Capitalism and Democracy

GW00634478

Morality, Capitalism and Democracy

Michael Novak

London
The IEA Health and Welfare Unit
1990

First published in 1990
by
The IEA Health and Welfare Unit
2 Lord North St
London SW1P 3LB

ISBN 0-255 36266-8

Typeset by the IEA Health and Welfare Unit
Printed in Great Britain by
Goron Pro-Print Co. Ltd
Churchill Industrial Estate, Lancing, West Sussex

Contents

Foreword

One of the more entrenched doctrines of our time is that capitalism is all about selfishness. Hand in hand with the notion that markets condone, even encourage, selfishness is the further assumption that socialism supplies the missing altruism. Attacking capitalism as selfish has always been part of the socialist strategy but it has assumed a particular prominence in recent times as leftists have begun to abandon their desire to control the economy through central planning. They now believe that the market is acceptable as the best means of creating wealth, so long as it is subordinated to socialist morality or 'social justice'.

No one has done more than Michael Novak to show that it is both false and reckless to caricature capitalism as a philosophy which condones selfishness. Nor is it true that socialists are the only altruists. Today's free societies have evolved from a rich philosophical tradition with three interlocking elements. First, 'democratic capitalism' offers an economic system, based on competition under law to channel self-interest into the service of others and to promote human creativity as the key to ending poverty. Second, it is a political system, emphasising constitutional checks and balances to protect ordered rights and to avoid the abuse of power. And third, it is also a moral and cultural system, inspired (in the West) by Greece and Rome, by Judaism and Christianity, by Renaissance and modern humanism—in short, a pluralistic, open, tolerant, but vital and dynamic ethos.

So frequently today, anyone who criticises the self-injuring or anti-social behaviour of others is described as authoritarian. Michael Novak makes plain that he does not want the law to enforce every moral rule that any one of us might personally prefer, but does insist that we should respect the necessity for vigourous moral debate without which a decent society is impossible. As John Stuart Mill wrote in *On Liberty*, 'Human beings owe to each other help to distinguish the better from the worse, and encouragement to choose the former and avoid the latter.' But

Mill also thought that there were other instruments 'to persuade people to their good than whips and scourges'.

The IEA never expresses a corporate view and disassociates itself from the views of its authors but Michael Novak is one of the foremost contributors to the developing classical-liberal tradition and we are honoured to be able to publish his lecture on 'Morality, Capitalism and Democracy', originally delivered at an IEA Health and Welfare Unit lecture in the Queen Elizabeth II Conference Centre. Michael Novak's essay is a succinct and authoritative re-statement of the ideals of the classical-liberal tradition which we commend to our readers in the hope that it will stimulate a long-overdue debate about the moral foundations of a free society. Democratic capitalism ought not to be dismissed as if it were morally stunted. On the contrary, it challenges the still-predominantly collectivist status quo, not only with an alternative political and economic theory, but also with a moral vision which is more than a match for any rival.

David G. Green

The Author

Michael Novak holds the George Frederick Jewett Chair in Religion and Public Policy at the American Enterprise Institute in Washington, D.C. He has written over twenty influential books in the areas of philosophy, theology, politics, economics and culture, including: *The Spirit of Democratic Capitalism* (1982), *Freedom with Justice: Catholic Social Thought and Liberal Institutions* (1984), *Will It Liberate? Questions about Liberation Theology* (1986) and *Taking Glasnost Seriously* (1988). He also wrote the text of the influential *New Consensus on Family and Welfare* (1987). His latest book is *Free Persons and the Common Good* (1989).

His articles and essays have been published in popular journals including *The New Republic, Commentary, Harpers, The Atlantic,* and *National Review.* 'Illusions and Realities', his twice-weekly column was syndicated nationally from 1976-1980. (It was a Pulitzer finalist in 1979.) His column 'Tomorrow and Tomorrow' appeared monthly in *National Review* from 1979 until 1986. In January 1989, *Forbes Magazine* began running his new column, 'The Larger Context'.

Mr Novak's writings have appeared in every major western language, and in Bengali, Korean and Japanese. *The Spirit of Democratic Capitalism* has been reprinted often in Latin America, and was published underground in Poland in 1986.

In March 1986, with the rank of ambassador, Mr Novak headed the U.S. Delegation to the Experts' Meeting on Human Contacts at the Conference on Security and Cooperation in Europe (a continuation of the Helsinki Accord negotiations). With Senate approval he was appointed, in January 1984, to the Board for International Broadcasting, the private corporation which governs Radio Free Europe and Radio Liberty.

Born in Johnstown, Pennsylvania, in 1933, Michael Novak is married with three children.

1 INTRODUCTION

The most distinguished marxist in the United States, Robert Heilbroner, has recently written,

> Less than seventy-five years after it officially began, the contest between capitalism and socialism is over: capitalism has won.[1]

Socialist writers, in America at least, are retreating to the language of what we call 'liberalism', while stretching it to cover as much as they can of their old convictions, such as the doctrine of 'positive liberty'. Meanwhile, so corrosive has been the anti-capitalist tradition of Western cultural élites that many of our citizens remain morally uneasy about the triumph of capitalism.

Resistance to capitalism has a long humanistic and religious pedigree. Many advocates of capitalism have correspondingly been anti-religious. They have argued that capitalism is a system morally superior to socialist regimes. On both counts—it seems clear—history has vindicated their judgement. But there is a need, now, apart from the arguments of the past, to look more deeply into the moral and religious resources of capitalism.

For we seem to have reached a new stage for discussing the first principles of political economy. At this stage, the issue is not so much capitalism v. socialism (an issue now settled), as a diagnosis of the true, vital and humanistic premises of capitalism. We urgently need these premises, in order to marshal them wisely in the social reforms yet to be undertaken. This task of reform is never-ending. And our primary task now is to get the first principles of political economy straight—the first principles of capitalism and democracy, and their moral and religious sources.

As the old cliché has it, the Americans and the British are separated by a common language—and nowhere more so than in discussions of political economy. I hope, therefore, that you will permit me to speak about the religious and moral foundations of democratic capitalism in a distinctively American way, even if it should at first offend your ears. I propose, first, to speak briefly of the American experience with 'the commercial republic', that is, a capitalist economy joined to a democratic republic. Second, and at

greater length, I would like to discuss some of the background
ideas of Judaism and Christianity which inspire and correct our
continuing (and often flawed) search for a humane and just
political economy. Third, I want to amend Isaiah Berlin's *Two
Concepts of Liberty* by setting forth a third concept—the more
genuine liberal concept, I believe, and too much neglected. I will
conclude by suggesting that this third concept of liberty sheds first
and useful light on the crucial problem of how we may better
come to the aid of the able-bodied poor.

About such matters, we Americans are, it is said, less ideolog-
ically complex than Europeans. So permit me to speak with
perhaps excessive plainness. And let me start at the beginning.

You can imagine the institutional shape of democratic capitalism
as a pyramid. (One such is displayed on the Seal of the United
States, on the back of the dollar bill, above the motto *'novus ordo
seclorum'*. At the left-hand corner of the pyramid is the limited
government of a democratic republic; opposite it, over at the right-
hand corner, the free economy.) This way of looking at things
suggests that the political system is not the whole of the social
system, and not even the uppermost, controlling part, but only one
limited yet crucial cornerstone of it. Similarly, the economy is not
the whole of the social system, but only an important and dynamic
part of it.

There is, moreover, a third part. On the aforementioned Seal,
for example, the top of the pyramid was left deliberately un-
completed, to represent the open-endedness of the moral-cultural
system, under the Eye of conscience or candour or Providence.
The summary content of this moral system is expressed in the
propositions of the Declaration of Independence ('We hold these
truths...') and summarized by Abraham Lincoln at Gettysburg in his
phrase about a nation 'conceived in liberty and dedicated to the
proposition that all men are created equal.'

In our conception, then, the system we call democratic capitalism
is constituted by three independent, yet interdependent, systems:
political, economic and cultural. When the system is healthy, these
three systems check and balance each other. We believe neither
in 'unfettered capitalism' nor in a managerial, dominating state nor

in a single, mandatory form of conscience. Our system is pluralistic, democratic and capitalist—each distinct part checking the other two. In a certain sense, priority goes to the moral-cultural system, which protects the ideals that animate the system as a whole, brings it under judgement for its manifest failings, and drives it forward.

The central ideas in this moral-cultural order spring historically from Jewish-Christian conceptions of the human person and human community. This does not mean that to participate fully in this order one needs to be a Jew or a Christian; indeed, our founders claimed to be building to the measure of 'the system of natural liberty' proper to all humans everywhere. Still, Jewish and Christian insights into human sinfulness and human dignity did, in fact, prevent our founders from being utopians. Our framers were further chastened by many sorry lessons they drew from attempts at republican government in Athens and Rome, and by the sober reflections of several key figures of the Anglo-American Enlightenment. This complex of restraining ideas often goes by the name of 'civic republicanism'—well discussed in a recent book by Thomas Pangle, *The Spirit of Modern Republicanism*.[2] The points I wish to make about theology are not, therefore, sectarian or even doctrinal. Rather, they have to do with a 'horizon', a way of seeing human reality both in its misery and in its beauty.

It is obvious that in the American approach to political economy, the thinking and the experience of England and Scotland loomed large. Yet the American framers were quite conscious, too, of their originality. It seems useful, in fact, to try to sketch briefly one salient difference between Britain and America even today, particularly in the way in which Americans have learned to perceive capitalism. Take, for example, a sentence by Raymond Plant in *Citizenship, Rights and Socialism* (Fabian Tract No. 531). Speaking of market systems, he writes,

It is foreseeable that those who enter with fewest resources will leave it with fewest.

Perhaps this sentence rings true in Britain—although even Professor Plant describes himself 'as someone who grew up in a very working-class area in Grimsby after the war'.[3] But it represents a sentiment most Americans emphatically would *not* voice. Most of us are, in fact, descended from 'those with fewest resources'—very poor immigrants—yet our starting places do *not* determine our outcomes. One working-class girl, who ended up working for CBS News and then in the White House, recently wrote of America in her best-selling book,

> This is the fairest place there ever was, it's wide open, and no one has cause for bitterness.[4]

That is an archetypical American sentiment.

In almost any setting in America, almost all members of an audience can remember the time when their family lived in poverty. Almost all know that their ancestors, if not they themselves, had for generations worked very hard in some other land and not gotten very far. Perhaps for this reason, in America we have never had a strong socialist movement. We have experienced little of the bitterness, sense of exclusion, and resentment on which such movements prosper. Indeed, one of our more famous leftwingers, economist Lester Thurow of the Massachusetts Institute of Technology, has insisted that no major writer in America today is a socialist.[5] We do have writers, though, who make the same appeal to 'positive freedom' as Raymond Plant does. But before treating of such matters perhaps I should dwell on some differences between Britain and America at a little greater length.

2 Democracy and Capitalism in America

According to Hannah Arendt, the early history of America demonstrated to the world that most of a nation's citizens need not forever be trapped in poverty; and thus generated for Europe what came to be called in the nineteenth century 'the social problem'.[6] As long as the world could believe that 'the poor ye shall always have with you', and that little or nothing could be done to alter their fate, there was no social problem. After the American experience, poverty became a scandal. Put otherwise, after at least one nation had put into effect 'the cause of the wealth of nations', economic development became a moral imperative for all.

I know that socialists are inclined to say that the new American type of economy was conceived in 'possessive individualism' and dedicated to the proposition that each man should pursue his own self-interest. (In Plant's dictum: 'Those who enter with fewest resources will leave with fewest'.) But that wasn't how Abraham Lincoln put it at Gettysburg. And, as we have seen, it isn't how Americans have experienced it. Our families knew that their forebears had worked hard overseas without prospering; then, working perhaps equally hard in America, they prospered—so this difference, they appreciated, did not spring from their own hands, but from the system of which they were a part. They knew themselves to be participating in a great social experiment. It was not a matter of one man or one family alone. It was a matter of system: the 'blessings of liberty' we have traditionally called it.

There is a further point. The primordial task of Americans was to build new communities. When the first pilgrims left Leyden for the New World, there were no inns awaiting them, no crops stored in barns, no homes, no churches. Together, they had to build these. From the beginning, the primary American task has been to build new communities. We have done this, and continue to do it, chiefly through self-help and mutual co-operation. The most salient fact that struck Tocqueville in 1831 was that Americans live and move and have their being in multiple associations. Even today,

Americans are almost always working with others. Most of us are up to our ears in committees. (Even our children before the age of nine already belong to more groups, take part in more activities, and go to more meetings than both parents together can drive them to.) Our favourite sports are team sports. From the days of the frontier on, we have always worked with others. We had to. As Tocqueville put it,

> Americans of all ages, all stations in life, and all types of disposition are forever forming associations. There are not only commercial and industrial associations in which all take part, but others of a thousand different types—religious, moral, serious, futile, very general and very limited, immensely large and very minute. Americans combine to give fetes, found seminaries, build churches, distribute books, and send missionaries to the antipodes. Hospitals, prisons, and schools take shape in that way. Finally, if they want to proclaim a truth or propagate some feeling by the encouragement of a great example, they form an association. In every case, at the head of any new undertaking, where in France you would find the government or in England some territorial magnate, in the United States you are sure to find an association.[7]

Along with this communitarian impulse, Americans have also always had to cherish self-reliance, enterprise, or in any case the self-starting individual. There was no alternative. No social order existed 'out there' to protect citizens; they had to construct community for themselves: first (as Tocqueville also noted) in villages, then in townships, slowly in counties, eventually in states, and only after 250 years in a single federal government.[8] For Americans, community and self-reliance go together. To be free is to delight in the risk-taking, chance and adventure of building new communities. Community may be the aim, but to get there some individual has to get things started. Without leaders, inertia rules.

Adam Smith's question concerning 'the cause of the wealth of nations' had a great effect on the US Constitution of 1787. What, in a single word, is that cause? In Latin, *caput*—wit, invention, discovery. In America, the first great piece of capitalist legislation was the Patent and Copyright clause of the Constitution. Isolation in a wilderness had already made American settlers practical and inventive; the Patent Clause was like a match igniting practical habits with the fire of interest. Indeed, the notion that ideas are the cause of the wealth of nations may be traced back through the very early emphasis of the colonists upon education and upon improvisation, tinkering, and the use of one's own wits.[9] If you are searching to learn *How the West Grew Rich*—to cite a useful book by Birdzell and Rosenberg[10]—the short answer is: invention. This is, for example, the single greatest difference in culture between Latin America and the United States: the early and sustained emphasis of the latter upon the tight connection between learning and practical achievement.[11] Abraham Lincoln was particularly sensitive to this connection.[12]

Finally, there is the fact that the framers of our Constitution were determined to defeat envy. While they characterised a full half of their social ideal as 'all men are created equal', they were careful to distinguish between equality under the law and 'an equal division of property'. For James Madison, the pursuit of the latter was 'a wicked project'.[13] By the endowments of nature, in their freedom to deploy their talents as they wish, and in their personal pursuit of happiness, each human is different from any other. To preserve these differences, inherent in human liberty, is the first task of justice and, hence, of government.[14]

To this day, Americans on the whole (intellectuals aside) are immune to appeals to envy, class struggle, and levelling.[15] The lowly garbageman would fight rather than foreclose the chance that his son might become as rich and successful as anybody else in the land; he will have little truck with state-managed outcomes. Whereas one gains the impression that Europeans would, on the whole, prefer to have less, so long as all receive approximately the same, most Americans by far would rather match their wits against their circumstances and keep open the possibility of extraordinary outcomes. Americans do not associate justice with equality of outcomes, but quite the opposite. They would find equality of outcomes unjust.

On the whole, Americans are not inclined to envy the rich; indeed, we rather enjoy their antics, their divorces, their temporary splendour and their fall. Social mobility among us is as likely to be downwards as upwards (the relatively untold story is the downward side). This churning mobility, upwards and downwards, is quite clearly visible in longitudinal studies of almost all individuals—and certainly of families—over time.[16] We *like* the rough correlation between effort and outcome. It is only rough. Chance, talent, and luck play a large part in American lives, but external factors such as these are remarkably indifferent to social starting places. The rough correlation between diligence and reward is so frequently visible as to be a source of much personal satisfaction in the daily work of most Americans.[17]

Perhaps at this point you will wish to raise searching questions about the homeless, the condition of African-Americans, and (a recent media preoccupation) 'growing inequality' as between the top and the bottom earnings quintiles. These are good questions, and good answers are available to those who inquire honestly. The achievement of our own social ideals is far from complete, and in their light it is fair for outsiders to criticise us as we also criticise ourselves.

In a word, we Americans see our experiment in democratic capitalism as a social experiment, open, incomplete, and always in need of reform. A fertile source for the moral dynamism implicit in this vision lies in the moral-cultural system suggested by the Eye of scrutinizing conscience depicted on the Seal of the United States, and to that system we now turn.

3 The Jewish, Christian and Humanistic Vision

Many theoreticians wish to argue that capitalism is merely a neutral system, a set of techniques, and that morality only enters into the picture in choosing the uses to which a capitalist system should be put. Daniel Bell, for example, argues in this way in *The Cultural Contradictions of Capitalism.*[18] The value incarnated in a capitalist economy, he says, is efficiency. It is possible to view matters in this way. I think, however, that there are more profound categories, and a deeper way of looking at things. A capitalist economy (like a democratic polity and a pluralist culture) has certain cultural preconditions. It cannot be made to work in just any culture at all, among people of just any sort of habits and desires. Indeed, the 'arguments for capitalism before its triumph' advanced by David Hume and Adam Smith were moral arguments.[19] In their attack upon the ethos of the prevailing pre-capitalist system, such writers focused precisely upon the moral superiority of capitalism compared to alternative regimes.

Jews and Christians, I think, may approach the choice among possible regimes in the following way. Suppose that for more than a thousand years a civilization has been tutored by Judaism and Christianity in a certain vision of human destiny, stressing in particular the root of human dignity in the *Imago Dei*, that is, that all humans have been created in the image of the Creator. Jefferson expressed this so: 'The God who gave us life gave us liberty'.[20] Man is most like God in being responsible for directing his own destiny—not being driven merely by instinct and internal laws as other creatures are, but able to be provident in his own regard.[21] Practically every story in the Bible focuses on what occurs in the mind and will of an individual. In one chapter, King David is faithful to his lord; in another, unfaithful; the suspense always consists in not knowing what it will be next. Supposing such long-held beliefs, how should humans go about designing *institutions* worthy of their own dignity and liberty? The history of the human race, to paraphrase Lord Acton, is the history of liberty. Differentiating the various spheres of life—political, economic and cultural—and finding institutions that empower humans to exercise their inalienable capacities for reflection and for choice would become, then, the main line of human institutional history. Even unbelievers within such a culture, I wish to argue, providing only that they accept the centrality of reflection and choice in a truly human life, are beneficiaries of the horizon so familiar to Christians and to Jews.

Indeed, as I see matters, the thinkers of the Enlightenment, including Hume and Smith, made a brave attempt to think through a way of 'grounding' such a horizon without any recourse to Jewish or Christian faith. Perhaps this attempt was necessary in practice, in order to break the grip of the *ancien regime*, including the vast agricultural holdings of the Catholic bishops, monasteries and orders. It was, I think, less necessary in the speculative order and, in any case, this Enlightenment Project appears not to have ended altogether happily. As Alasdair MacIntyre puts it in *After Virtue*, the misconceived search for abstract philosophical certitude appears to have ended in the mutual shouting of epithets between one school and another—in a subjectivism far distant from the certain, universal, inescapable rational grounding that *les philosophes* had once imagined possible.[22]

However that may be, let us try to go back again in inquiry to that common horizon in which it was imagined that what is most precious in humans is the human capacity to reflect and to choose. How shall one construct a social order that will maximize their daily acts of reflection and choice? How shall one shape a *novus ordo* in such a way that in all the great spheres of life—political, economic, and moral-cultural—the frequency of personal acts of reflection and choice will be maximized? One condition of this search needs also to be specified: in this capacity for reflection and choice, all humans are created equal—not in the sense that their talents are the same, but in the sense that each is ultimately responsible for his or her own destiny (or personal pursuit of happiness). From this point of view, the search for a *novus ordo* is a search for an arrangement of social institutions worthy of human capacities for reflection and choice.

Further, the horizon derived from Jewish and Christian history suggests four further themes fruitful for investigation: human fallibility and sin; human creativity; community; and a specific understanding of liberty. Each of these themes affects our conception of institutions likely to work successfully in practice.

1. *Human fallibility and sin*

The whole panorama of human history suggests that utopian thinking is fraught with the danger of tyranny. If every human sometimes sins—and experience seems to show, alas, that each of us does—then no human being is to be trusted with total power. To every ambition, it will seem wise to institutionalise a counter-ambition. A political system that would secure the liberty and equality of all before the law will have to empower, first, a limited government and, second, a government with many in-built checks and balances. If men were angels, this would not be necessary; but we are not angels and precautions are needed.[23]

More even than this, a limited government will also have to be protected against the diseases to which *democracy* is prey, including the propensity of democracies to trample on the rights of individuals and minorities. Further still, the political power will have to be separated by some important degree from power over the economic decision making of individuals and groups. Yet further, the political power will have to be separated from power over conscience, ideas and information.

In brief, in order to maintain the liberty of reflection and choice in all three major spheres of life—political, economic, and moral-cultural—the overwhelming persistence of human fallibility and sinfulness will counsel the effective separation of all three major systems of power into mutually independent hands. While there must needs be (and will inevitably be) élites in all three spheres, no one of these élites—political, economic, or moral-cultural—is wholly to be trusted. (In the United States, we encapsulate this counsel thus: 'In God we trust'—meaning, in 'no one else'.)

2. Creativity

As the Creator made every human in His image, imparting to each a vocation to be creative, so each human has an inalienable right to personal economic initiative or enterprise.[24] Each human being has a capacity to create more during a lifetime than he or she consumes; this is the principle that makes human economic development possible. This personal creativity, the very principle of economic progress, calls forth in humans the need to identify in themselves, to cherish, and to nurture the virtue of enterprise—that is, the intellectual capacity to discern and to discover new possibilities, and the moral capacity to realise these possibilities in fact.[25]

In the surrounding social system experience shows that this inalienable right requires for its fruitful exercise a regime of private property; ease of legal incorporation; the protection of patents and copyrights; and access to credit—and that such requirements must be made available also for those born poor or of modest family origin. Hernando de Soto's *The Other Path*, for example, shows how these basic requirements still are lacking in the Third World. De Soto demonstrates that the overwhelming proportion of the poor in Peru (and elsewhere) are neither peasants nor proletarians but entrepreneurs, even though their entrepreneurial activities are presently regarded by the state as criminal.[26]

3. Community

In the pre-modern world, community was typically organic and holistic, accompanied quite often by xenophobia, intolerance, and minimal regard for personal rights even within the bonded community. But this ancient word 'community' necessarily acquires a new shape and new meaning in a world intent upon honouring capacities of personal reflection and choice as the seats of human dignity. When it includes respect for personal capacities of reflection and choice, even the relatively new word 'solidarity', favoured by socialists and (in a somewhat different sense) by Pope John Paul II,[27] carries a new shape and meaning. When solidarity includes respect for liberty of conscience, it has a much fuller and more complex significance than it once had in simpler, more tribal, and less pluralistic contexts. The sort of solidarity available in working-class Grimsby just before and after World War II that Raymond Plant mentions is, as Plant rightly notes, neither quite so available nor so obviously attractive and legitimate today.[28]

Today, then, those communities are held to be more legitimate that respect and nourish the capacities for reflection and choice of all the persons within them. On the one hand, individual persons require community for the full development of their capacities for reflection and choice; on the other hand, communities today are judged by their capacity to empower a flowering of reflection and choice among their members.[29] These are high standards on both counts. They place considerable strain on all our institutions—and on all our citizens.

It is further important to note that the most distinctive invention of democratic capitalist systems is not the possessive individual; it is the voluntary association and the corporation. Nearly all tasks today, especially economic tasks, are too large and too complex for one individual alone or even for one generation alone. Thus, new social institutions have had to be invented that would permit individuals voluntarily to enter into association with others. Many of these social institutions—associations, corporations—have a legal standing that enables them to bridge the generations in social institutions that persist much longer than the individual lifetimes of those who voluntarily join them. Further, this legal standing makes these new associations and corporations independent of the state. They are social, but not statist.

A great proportion of the hours of our lives today are spent within such social bodies. We do not live and move and have our being as rugged individuals solely, nor solely as members of the state, but in free and cooperative association with our fellows in a large profusion of social institutions. Accordingly, the social skills of individuals within democratic capitalist societies must be—and in fact are—very highly developed.

Under this heading, too, I want to comment on one aspect of markets that theoreticians commonly neglect: markets draw individuals out of isolation and into reasoned, civil, voluntary interchange with their fellows. As Max Weber often noted in his historical researches, 'city air makes free', markets 'bustle', and market behaviour serves as a great transmitter of new knowledge, new skills and stimulating exposure to wider worlds.[30]

Moreover, markets have a centripetal force; their inner dynamic aims at mutual, civil, reasoned agreements. Markets do not drive people apart into alienation; on the contrary, they drive them toward closer contact with one another, even from the antipodes. Markets are extraordinary social institutions, rich with tacit understandings, traditions, conventions, and valuable lore. Open to the world, they bind humans together in thousands of visible and invisible filaments of choice. They are one of the great works of human reason, all the more remarkable for not being guided by any single human reason and for not being transparent to or manageable by any single person or group of persons. Markets are a permanent rebuff to the rationalistic conceit, which would reject whatever reason cannot master top-down.[31]

From a purely libertarian point of view, of course, many philosophers approach the questions of democracy and capitalism solely from individualistic premisses. For Jews or Christians, this viewpoint is insufficient. From a Jewish and Christian point of view, the human community, communities of faith, families, and even nations or peoples, are important—even prior—realities. Given the fact that building a *novus ordo* on a democratic, capitalist and pluralistic foundation is a preeminently social task, I see no reason to surrender the concept of community to socialists. It is not by the protection of the rights of individuals alone that democratic capitalist societies commend themselves to the fair and impartial judgement of humankind. They do so also by the kinds of social institutions they generate and by the kinds of communities they form. Indeed, the most significant inventions of democratic capitalist societies have been new kinds of social institutions.

It is one of the ironies of our century that the great socialist societies have ended by privatizing the lives of their own populations, souring them, embittering them; whereas democratic capitalist societies, which talk so much about the individual, have inspired in their citizens considerable love for such social realities as systems, institutions, and local communities. One may suppose that this is because democratic capitalist societies expend so many efforts keeping the space of civic life open and alive, so that within it many social energies may thrive and even boil. Possessive individuals? I should say that the empirical picture is, rather, of lively and engaged associational individuals, even communitarian individuals, who enjoy both cooperation and solitude, each in its due season.

4. *Liberty*

The idea of socialism, it seems, has been dying the death of a thousand tiny (and not so tiny) qualifications; the death of the socialist idea was (even before the dramatic events of 1989) one of the most under-reported facts of our era.[32] To the extent that this is true, the democratic capitalist idea of liberty is in ascendancy. One result is that socialists are now rushing to appropriate the word 'liberty' (and its correlatives such as 'rights'). In reaching for this flag, however, socialists must attempt to re-define it to their own purposes. Those purposes seem always to entail both increments of state power and a diminishment of personal dignity. Since these are complex issues, I will need a larger space for their discussion.

4 A Third Concept of Liberty

Theologically, it is important to distinguish among various conceptions of liberty. Not all theories of liberty qualify as 'Christian
liberty'. Some socialist writers in Britain and America wish to
argue, for example, that 'bourgeois liberal' liberty is purely
'negative', that is, constituted by the absence of external constraint.
By contrast, they wish to assert, a socialist conception of liberty is
'positive', that is, constituted by a grant of the means necessary to
exercise liberty, such as education or income.[33] Both these
conceptions fall short of the Christian—and, I should say, classical—conception. The first errs by being external to the self and
far too broad. The American framers conceived of liberty as
'ordered liberty', requiring for its exercise a degree of manly or
womanly strength (*virtus*) sufficient to achieve internal self-mastery
over one's passions and appetites, so as to judge matters as coolly,
realistically and dispassionately as reflection and deliberate choice
require. In this sense, liberty is contrasted with license; ordered
liberty with the disordered passions; and self-mastery with slavery
to one's passions or appetites. 'Ordered liberty' is no mere absence
of external constraint. On the contrary, it requires for its coming
into being a quite considerable internal restraint. An American
hymn catches this splendidly:

> Confirm thy soul in self-control
> Thy liberty in law.

In brief not *any* act free from external constraint ensures liberty,
nor can a merely negative liberty qualify as the real thing.

   I know that Isaiah Berlin makes much of this contrast in his *Two
Concepts of Liberty*, and that he identifies the negative concept
with the liberal tradition, and the positive concept with aspirations
toward collectivism and totalitarianism.[34] It is just possible that his
concept of negative liberty makes some sense as an analytical tool,
while being quite inadequate as a guide to classical liberalism as an
historical movement. Most liberal thinkers from Locke onwards

had more in mind for liberty than the mere (negative) protection the rights of the individual against the power of the state. Certainly, Berlin's analysis does not quite work for the American tradition.

What Professor Berlin fears is that any attempt to add positive content to the purely negative concept of liberty will awaken the fatal desire to suppress those who fall short of the preferred positive definition. But is this necessarily the case? Suppose that one cherishes a *political* concept of liberty—the negative concept—such that the state may make no law regarding the free exercise of conscience. It will not violate this concept if one cherishes, in addition, a *moral* concept of liberty, but without seeking to impose it by law upon others. In this sense, by persuasion and education one upholds liberty as a moral ideal to be freely appropriated by each citizen.

Indeed, this moral concept seems even to be necessary to the political concept. For it is highly doubtful whether any regime could long maintain the political concept of liberty, unless its citizens voluntarily and willingly accepted the disciplines and constraints of an internalised regime rather like that of 'ordered liberty'. Unless citizens are capable of exercising self-government over their own interests, passions, prejudices, and lusts for power and advantage, it is highly probable that they will not for long be capable of maintaining political self-government. For that difficult task, considerable moral virtue is prerequisite. In fact, a society without civic virtue would be uncivilised, perhaps even dramatically barbaric.

True liberty, therefore, requires habituation to quite considerable moral skills, including temperance, courage, just judgement and practical wisdom. In the ordinary case, liberty is not merely given, but has to be acquired through painstaking discipline, until its constituent habits become 'second nature'. This is the liberty that Jefferson—and, indeed, the liberal tradition generally—had in mind, at least implicitly. Lord Acton expressed it quite well as 'the liberty to do not what we like but what we ought'.[35]

I should like to emphasise, further, that the exercise of this liberty entails that a man should take responsibility for his own actions. To be a free man is to stand under judgement—judgement by one's own conscience, by the conscience of an 'impartial spectator' or 'objective observer', by history, and by the Almighty. For to act freely, as the master of one's own acts, is to act with full reflection and sufficient deliberation—that is, not merely from inadvertence, by physical reflex, or aimlessly. Absentmindedly nudging sand with one's toe at the beach is not a deliberate act. To act with reflection and deliberation is, then, to be accountable for one's acts—but also for the realism of one's judgements. For others will surely point out such illusions as distort our behaviour in their regard.

In the genuine liberal conception of liberty, therefore, free actions spring from calm and reflective judgements about truth. This is, for certain, the Jewish and Christian conception of liberty—as in the text, 'The truth shall make you free' (John 8:32). This is far more than a 'negative' conception; it arises from specific internally derived constraints and standards. This is the liberty that is at the root of human autonomy, responsibility and dignity, and that enables the creature to act in the image of the Creator.

There is, then, if I am right about all this, a third concept of liberty neglected by Professor Berlin. Without developing it fully here, let me link it to Acton's conception of liberty as 'the reign of conscience'.[36] This conception has both classical and Christian roots. Its essential note is that whoever has liberty has responsibility, and that this responsibility is fixed by personal conscience, by the impartial judgement of other humans, and by the judgement of God. There are echoes in Acton's concept of John Locke's discussion of education for liberty,[37] as well as of Adam Smith's discussions of civic humanism, sympathy and the impartial spectator.[38] Tocqueville adverted to it in discussing the American conception of liberty, which followed Cotton Mather in distinguishing between the liberty to do what one desires (license) and the liberty to do what one ought to do in the light of the laws of nature and of nature's God (ordered liberty).[39] In these ways, Acton's conception goes beyond Berlin's first concept, negative liberty, by highlighting those conditions of liberty that are internal to the free person. It might be thought of as a variant of Berlin's second concept of liberty, positive liberty. But what Berlin objects to in the concept of positive liberty is its tendency to expand into coercive arrangements, whereas Acton's concept is explicitly designed to protect personal responsibility from any scheme of coercion by others.

Acton's conception of liberty as personal responsibility is, therefore, quite rich. Without being limited to, it draws upon specifically Jewish and Christian materials. In his surveys of historical materials, Acton finds that this concept of liberty does not 'subsist' outside of cultures radically affected by Christianity.[40] In its roots, this liberty is more moral than political.[41] For its roots lie in the inalienable liberty of each human person, responsible for his immortal soul before the judgement of God, a responsibility no other person can possibly alienate from him. Nonetheless, to be able to enjoy the free exercise of this liberty, a human being requires the blessings of a sufficiently developed culture and a wisely articulated set of political institutions.[42] History shows well enough that the free exercise of this natural liberty is often trampled on and abridged by an inhospitable culture or an oppressive political system.

In sum, liberty in Acton's conception has both a moral and a political dimension; that is, both a highly personal and a fully social context. In the first of these dimensions, individuals must individually conquer and appropriate this liberty for themselves. It is their vocation and their destiny to make a pilgrim's progress in the painstaking (and often lonely) appropriation of their own responsibility. In the second of these dimensions, human societies and cultures—in their efforts to become more and more worthy of the inalienable dignity of their own citizens—must constantly invent institutions able to expand and, as it were, to allow air and space for the flowering of this liberty among their citizens. In this dimension, liberty is a socio-historical project, as in the first it is a personal vocation. Thus, to establish the reign of liberty politically is to secure throughout human affairs the free working of personal conscience.

It may be objected to Acton that a society that permits complete liberty of conscience must necessarily be anarchic and anomic, just as it is objected to Adam Smith that liberty in personal economic initiative must also lead to anarchy. To this, Smith's counter was that economic activities by their nature must bend to the economic preferences of others. Thus, each individual decisionmaker is led toward cooperation with others by the centripetal force inherent in his need to reach a reasoned agreement with other free agents. This in-built drive toward mutually agreeable exchange is a powerful inducement to mutual adjustment and cooperation. One man's economic purposes can only be secured by voluntary cooperation with many others in rule-based, reasoned activities. Analogously, those who defend Acton's commitment to personal, moral and religious liberty point to centripetal drives inherent in the laws of nature and of nature's God. The highest expression of moral liberty is friendship for one another. Only a little lower on the moral scale is a voluntary deference to and respect for the God-given dignity of every other human being. In a word, there is nothing inherent, either in economic liberty or in moral liberty, that must drive individuals to anarchy, anomie, lawlessness, or nihilism. On the contrary, many reasons inhere in both economic liberty and moral liberty that drive individuals to mutual respect for and freely chosen cooperation with others.

It remains true, of course, that liberty of any sort—economic, moral or political—is subject to human sinfulness. Sin, in this context, means *aversio a Deo*, that is, a freely chosen course of separation from God, from reason, from cooperation with others, and from respect for the dignity of others.[43] Humans do sin. That is why no human society can be constructed on the supposition that its members are angels, saints, or free from sin. From this derives a political corollary—sin is the reason why checks and balances are necessary. Sin is the reason why every form of social power—the power of one man over another—must be divided, limited, checked and hemmed around with 'auxiliary precautions'.[44] Because of sin, the project of building a genuinely free society, truly respectful of human dignity, and especially of the dignity of the most vulnerable, is long, painstaking, often ironical and frequently counter-intuitive.[45] Sin is a surd in human society.[46] The widespread and obvious fact of sin stands as an impediment to every merely rationalistic conception of society. Perhaps it is wise to dwell on this point for a moment.

Try to imagine a world without sin. In such a world, the clear light of basic concepts and ideals would have compelling force. In such a utopia, it may seem obvious to some that all human ideals would be in harmony with one another. It may even seem obvious to them that there are shortcuts to securing the common good of all—perhaps by some beneficent and simple system of command. In a utopian world, both leaders and followers would be reasonable. This is the source of the rationalist conceit.

But the moment that we would try to apply this idea of the harmony of all human ideals in this actual and less perfect world, there would follow a scheme for enforcing this harmony upon recalcitrant and sinful individuals in the name of social justice. The next step would be an even worse delusion, namely, that some human beings somewhere have sufficient knowledge to remake all our institutions from scratch. This élite would then invent a rationalistic scheme for organising human society through some shorter route than reliance upon the autonomy of individual consciences. Hayek calls this 'the fatal conceit'.[47] This conceit necessarily gives rise to political gnosticism, that is, to the need to rely upon some specially chosen corps of the enlightened, some constituency of conscience, some vanguard of social justice, some leading cadre of those whose consciences have been raised above those of their more errant and benighted brothers. In religion, this conceit has led to the Inquisition; in morals, to the reign of the saints; in politics to the gulag; and in economics to the command economy. This conceit leads to monism, not pluralism.

Christian liberty begins, by contrast, in the sharp and reasoned awareness of human sinfulness and fallibility. In the very name of this Christian liberty, Christians (and others) must resist the premature enforcement of the Kingdom of God—the reign of social justice—upon earth. Acton's 'reign of conscience' cannot be achieved through coercion. Any effort to do so would forfeit its claim to represent liberty of conscience, and also its claim to be Christian. The only way open to the genuine advancement of liberty—it is by no means an inefficacious way—is indirect, requiring much patience and mutual forbearance. Positively, that way is by education, reasoned persuasion, and appeal to 'the better angels of our nature'. Negatively, that way is by the strict limitation of all social powers, their division into many different and competing hands, the counterbalancing of every ambition by a rival ambition, and those other practical devices of checks and balances that are arrived at through historical trial and error.

There are two dangers in pointing out that liberty is not merely negative but, rather, requires for its practical exercise concrete actions such as reflecting (i.e., seeking reasons) and choosing. The first danger lies in imagining that there is only *one* right way to reflect and choose. A second danger lies in objectifying this monism in the social order, so that in the name of 'true liberty' moral coercion would come to rule. All religious movements, Christianity included, are prone to these temptations, as are such secular cults of 'solidarity' and 'social justice' as Marxist-Leninism. So is a purely empty secular liberalism, smilingly nihilistic, which would leave liberty intellectually defenseless.

By contrast, the third concept of liberty articulates the internal dynamics of the exercise of liberty. These consist (at least) in seeking reasons and forming decisions (choices). For liberty is not merely extrinsic to the free person; it is an ordered engagement of particular activities of consciousness. In exercising liberty, the human being is not merely not being coerced by others but is also acting in specific modalities: not absent-mindedly but reflectively; not indiscriminately but deliberately. To act in such ways is no mean achievement; to do so frequently requires specific (and admirable) habits. Since to exercise liberty is to perform such admirable acts as to reflect and to choose, liberty is not merely 'negative'. But, then, neither is it 'positive' in the sense that sets off alarms, since in order to highlight (even in one's own consciousness) the activities of reflecting and choosing, one need not specify the content of reflections and choices. To Berlin's two questions about liberty, therefore, I would add a third. To 'Who is master?' and 'Over what area am I master?' must be added, 'How is mastery over one's actions exercised?'

Clearly, the progress of liberty in human persons and societies is most reliable when it is concrete, enmeshed with intelligently judged human experience, and acquired by self-reforming trial-and-error. The pursuit of liberty is a dynamic internal force, proceeding as it were from a living mustard seed, which by its vital energy commands attention to the immediate necessities of its flourishing and rejects those environments hostile to it. The nurturing of the seed of liberty in every human heart is the supreme art of human living. It is the work of practical wisdom. To come to the support of liberty, cognate arts must be learned in every sphere into which the human race deploys institutions—political wisdom, economic wisdom and moral-cultural wisdom.

5 Christian vs. Socialist Liberty

Although Isaiah Berlin's presentation of the liberal conception of liberty as 'negative' falls short of reality, the presentation of 'positive freedom' by certain socialists of our own day does fall heir to his objections. If I understand the matter correctly, the new socialist tendency is to embrace the goal of liberty (no longer dismissing it as 'bourgeois liberty') and then to redefine it. This new socialist definition holds that liberty is a 'capacity', and thus can be invoked, again the old socialist effort to equalise such 'capacities' for all. In this way, socialist equality is once again enthroned above liberty. People who are unequal in capacity, it is said, are unequally free, and this inequality is wrong. Why is this way of thinking incorrect?

For one thing, to say that those who are illiterate and unlearned face a narrower range of choices than do the literate and learned is merely a truism. One of the justifications for undergoing the disciplines of education, particularly of the liberal ('liberating') arts, is precisely to broaden one's horizons of choice. For another thing, there is a very great difference between an illiterate, unlearned man who lives under harsh tyranny, and his cousin who has migrated to dwell under a free regime. The first devoutly aspires to liberty but his way is blocked. The second, equally unlearned and illiterate, is now in a position to use such opportunities as are freely arrayed before him to broaden his horizons and to grow in his capacities for yet further liberties. Although both are equal in internal capacities, the first lives in an unfree social order, the second in a free one.

Precisely at this point there seems to be a difference of perception between partisans of equality and partisans of liberty. Those most inclined to the socialist dream seem to be offended by unequal capacities and unequal performances, and would like to equalise them. In the past, the banner under which they marched was 'Equality'. They now have a new banner: 'Liberty'. But what they mean by this is 'equality in capacities'. It is the old battlecry, in fresh syllables. It is meant to suggest that if individuals do not have the same capacities as others, they are not in those respects free.

By contrast, the American framers wished jealously to protect the 'unequal faculties' which they observed among men; such inequality was to them no scandal. They would have thought it tyranny to attempt to eliminate those inequalities. So contrary to nature would such suppression be, they thought, that only a very thorough tyranny indeed could be expected to impose it. The Lord God Himself distributes unequally His talents and gifts. Nature is not egalitarian. Nor is human liberty—given exactly the same talents, two persons will use them differently. Indeed, so strongly did the American framers feel about these differences, and so fundamental to liberty did they judge them to be, that they spoke emphatically of the basic right to 'life, liberty and *the pursuit of happiness*'. Human beings do not seek identity, and they do not seek equality, when they pursue happiness. They pursue whatever it is that they freely choose. Their idiosyncrasies and irrepressible varieties inevitably destroy the best laid plans of planners. Written into human personality is not equality but liberty.

An anecdote may illustrate the sense in which the pursuit of happiness frustrates equality. Consider twin sisters born in Iowa, but working as successful professional women on similar incomes in New York. Emily is a frugal saver, prudent householder, and studious investor. Since neither sister is married, her sister Charlotte sees no reason whatever to save, and loves fine clothes, elegant dining, and expensive vacations in faraway places. At the age of 65, Emily, lucky in her mutual fund investments, retires with $1.2 million in her brokerage account, but worries about her sister Charlotte, who has barely $1,000 to her name. Observing these two sisters, an egalitarian may find any system unfair that allows one person (Emily) to amass wealth more than 1,000 times greater than another (Charlotte). But it is Charlotte who feels sorry for Emily—Emily may have the money, but Charlotte has the memories. Thus do unequal choices in the pursuit of happiness place liberty at loggerheads with equality.

But let us return to a plainer sense of the phrase, 'the free society'. On this planet of 165 or so nations, only a few nations offer to the illiterate and unlearned political and civil liberties and economic opportunity; most of the others keep their citizens in civic, political, and economic bondage. This difference warrants a significant distinction between free men and subjects. However equal in their misery whole multitudes might be, even the illiterate and the unlearned recognize and cherish this difference, migrating by the millions from places that are unfree.

Yes, some used to respond (prior to 1989), but in the Communist parts of Eastern Europe, even the poorest citizens are guaranteed a job, income, housing, food and medical care. Does this not constitute a kind of freedom superior to that of the unemployed, homeless, impoverished poor person in Washington, D.C? In Washington, there are prisons that supply all material necessities for their inmates but, however humanely cared for, we do not call such inmates free. Full material care and freedom are not the same. Moreover, as Eastern Europe's experiment with socialism shows, those who would offer bread first, liberty later, run the risk of failing to produce either. What most men and women seem to want, if migration patterns are any indication, is the liberty to provide for their own necessities in a land of opportunity. Such social opportunity is the key to human dignity.

If I understand them correctly, socialists would like to offer more than a regime of civic and political liberties, significant as the democrats among them recognize these liberties to be. They want to offer something more than material security: a passable equality in capacities. They do not recognize the opposition between equality and liberty. When equality entails a requirement to seek identity in capacities, talents, energies, purposes, initiatives, actions, and outcomes, it is wholly incompatible with personal liberty, with the admirable diversity of actual talents, and with the individual pursuit of happiness. Moreover, when the achievement of a regime of equality is the stated aim of central power, equality becomes the dreadful enemy of liberty—it is, as James Madison called it, a 'wicked project'.[48]

This intellectual error (and error of the heart as well) arises in three steps. First, the socialists confound the ordered liberty of the liberal society with the ordered equality (identity) of the socialist society of their dreams. Although they try to force liberal arguments to do socialist work, ordered liberty is incompatible with socialist equality. Second, socialists fail to recognize that it is characteristic of human persons to have unequal personal capacities (abilities, dispositions) and, consequently, unequal possession of the fruits of human action (the ownership of properties of various kinds). This failure of insight leads them to imagine that in a just society all persons would enjoy equal capacities and equal possessions. In fact this ideal could only hold true if every person had identical natural endowments, purposes, energies, and choices—if persons were not free to take risks, to choose differently, etc. This ideal is incompatible with the exercise of human liberties. Third, socialists wrongly assign to the state the task of making human persons identical in their capacities and possessions, whether they choose to be identical or not.

In these three ways, the socialist ideal seems incompatible with a free and diverse society. If so, this would account for the recognized sameness and greyness of socialist experiments, from which liberty has been excised. Moreover, the logic of identity is quite insatiable. How can incomes be equal if talents are not? Will not unusual strength of arm, good looks, or an exceptional voice result in unequal outcomes? Will not luck itself be distributed on an unfair basis? Short of an absolute tyranny, how could concrete individual differences be equalized? And why would that be regarded as morally admirable? In the implicit logic of socialism, it seems, the word 'equality' approximates 'identity'. No one, perhaps, follows this logic through to the end. But it is a logic to be wary of in its beginnings.

Moreover, the pursuit of the socialist ideal involves the following paradox. The more a socialist regime attempts to impose equality, the more it deprives human persons of personal responsibility. Put otherwise, the more it tries to redistribute the fruits of liberty so as to equalize outcomes, the more it severs the ligaments of personal responsibility for the development of one's own capacities and the achievement of one's own desired outcomes. By regarding all persons as subjects of equalization by state authority—as victims of some putative injustice—it in effect regards its citizens as passive and dependent. It cuts the link between personal purpose and personal achievement, in order to secure its own rational purposes. Citizens became pawns of a 'new soft despotism', 'soft' only in the sense that it claims to be taking action solely for the good of its subjects.

By contrast, the Christian view of the inequalities inherent in human personality—in a diversity of gifts and talents, under Providence—sets upon all human creatures the same command: Become all that you can become, 'as perfect as our heavenly Father is perfect', but with the understanding that each single person is utterly unlike any other. Each needs to do all each can. It is as singular individuals that we will be judged, not as identical units. 'By their fruits you shall know them.' 'In my father's house there are many mansions.' Etc.

It is important here to avoid confusion between two quite different aims of social policy. It is quite right to wish to come to the support of the poor, the vulnerable, the disabled and others who are (temporarily or permanently) unable to provide for their own necessities. It does not follow that the good society should expunge all diversity, variety, and inequality either of gifts or of outcomes.

The Christian view of liberty holds quite clearly that each free person is 'his brothers keeper', and that the hungry should be fed, the naked clothed, and the like. Each society, by Christian standards, is to be judged morally by how well it cares for its most vulnerable members. To do this, it is not necessary to accept the doctrine of 'positive freedom', that is, the achievement of social identity through dependency upon the power of the state. On the contrary, one must keep in mind the law of human dignity. Made in the image of Divine Providence, each able-bodied person is responsible for becoming provident on his or her own behalf, and master of his or her own needs. It is the task of the good society to empower able-bodied citizens to do this, but in such a way that the state does not do it for them, thus taking away their personal responsibility and personal dignity.

Wherever through illness, disability, or misfortune individuals are overwhelmed by greater difficulties than they can master, it is entirely proper for others to come to their assistance. Ideally the front line of such assistance ought to arise from the free will and civic spirit of their families, neighbours, and fellow citizens, acting more or less independently of the state. When such resources fall short, and as a last resort, it is proper to turn to the state: local first, then regional, then national.

We Catholics call this 'the principle of subsidiarity',[49] according to which problems should be solved at the most local and concrete level, closest to personal responsibility, and at higher levels of social organization only when the lower cannot succeed. The reasoning behind this principle is twofold: to protect both the principle of personal responsibility and the concrete connection with the particulars of the case, on the one hand, and, on the other, to provide checks against the tendencies of state power to render individuals and local communities subject to distant authorities and excessively dependent upon them. Obviously, such a principle allows for the utmost diversity. It also works against the confusion of equality with identity.

In brief, I much prefer the third concept of liberty—the concept that binds liberty tightly to personal responsibility—to the 'positive freedom' propounded by the newer socialists. I prefer it as morally superior, politically more sound, more efficacious in public policy, and more likely to produce both the public and the private good.

6 Some Practical Lessons for Today

If I have so far been right in the drift of my argument—right about
the American idea of 'ordered liberty', right about the Jewish and
Christian sources of certain central modern impulses in political
economy, and right about the third concept of liberty—what
lessons may be briefly drawn for guidance in our current social
perplexities? I will limit myself to one such.

There seems to be a widespread and admirable impulse—in
America, Britain, and throughout the world—to worry about how
our societies can better care for the most vulnerable in our midst:
the homeless, the hungry, the unemployed, the ill and disabled, the
elderly, the unskilled, the disoriented, the poor. Raymond Plant in
effect, in his earlier cited Fabian Tract, defines this task as moving
from negative liberty to positive liberty—from the absence of
constraint to the 'improvement' of the capacities of the poor.
Professor Berlin worries about the authoritarianism lurking in this
second concept of liberty, and indeed one can see in Plant's brave
effort to redefine socialism for our time a bit too much of the old
socialism. Its foreseeable result is the creation of what Belloc
would perhaps have called a rather large servile class, wholly
dependent upon the state.[50] Tocqueville, too, warned against the
all-smothering, need-supplying, profligately 'compassionate' and
'caring' state. The problems of the needy and the vulnerable are
all too real. One must take care in meeting them not to create a
disease worse than the present necessity.

Our earlier reflections, I would like to think, suggest a better
way. To reach it, it is crucial to fix our end clearly in mind. In the
name of compassion, many grievous sins have been committed.
The legend of the Grand Inquisitor displays one of them. An old
Tammany Hall saying displays another: 'The fella that said
patriotism is the last refuge of scoundrels underestimated the
possibilities of compassion.' Our aim is not, must not be, merely to
demonstrate our own compassion. That would be self-referential,
and might disguise a subtle lust for tyranny over others. Our aim
must be to liberate the poor; that is, to enable them to appropriate

their own liberty—to become independent, self-reliant, autonomous, free citizens.

For some of the most vulnerable, of course, the achievement of such independence will not be possible. Some are too young, too old, too ill, too disabled, or otherwise unable to achieve the independence proper to healthy adulthood, and are necessarily dependent upon others. The rest of us must come quickly and generously to their assistance. By the principle of subsidiarity, it would be far better if our method of organizing this assistance were to strengthen 'the little platoons' to which these needy ones already belong: their families, friends, neighbours, and associates. Our laws and our methods of social assistance should be designed, as much as possible, to assist smaller, local communities to care for them with the sort of attention to particular detail that only those who know them well are in a position to administer. It must be a last resort—sadly, alas, often necessary—to assist them wholesale, as it were, in large collective schemes administered by the state. For want of an alternative, this latter must be done, even though its administrative difficulties and the diseases inherent in them are by now well known. About these necessarily dependent ones there is not, I think, much controversy, except the inevitable and incessant ones over administrative methods, new inspirations, and reforms.

More touching to the human heart—and perplexing to social workers everywhere—are those rather large numbers of able-bodied persons who could be independent, but for one reason or another are not. Here the task of giving assistance becomes quite paradoxical. Clearly, such persons do need assistance; yet assistance badly given may increase, rather than alleviate, their dependency. If our aim is to help such persons to appropriate their own liberty, we would falsify that purpose were we inadvertently to ensnare them in perpetual dependency. How to move such persons from dependency to independence is not always clear or, even when clear, easy to accomplish. Nonetheless, if our self-proclaimed aim is liberty—and nothing less is worthy of their dignity or ours—that is the transition necessary to accomplish. Without it, there is no real civic community. There is only a nation half free, half servile; half free-standing and independent, half mired in dependency.

A language often heard in this connection today is that we need 'to empower the poor to participate in the decisions that affect their lives.' Those excluded from these decisions are said to be 'marginalized'. Such language betrays a preference for an image of civic society as a collectivist apparatus, in which collective decisions are taken. My reason for resistance to such language is not its socialist provenance. Rather, it is that such an image masks the true nature of a civic community. A civic community is characterized by reasoned discourse; it is established on the ground that each of its members is capable of reflection and choice, and thus inalienably responsible for his or her destiny. Each is a creative source of initiative—moral, political, economic. A good society must give ample space to this initiative. The provision of ample opportunities about which personal decisions are taken is far more central to empowerment than is 'participation in collective decisions'.

To be sure, the contribution of each citizen is needed by the whole community. Each should not only be receiving benefits from the community but should also be contributing to the whole community, and gaining an essential satisfaction therefrom. To effectuate this state of affairs, ways need to be found—imagined and invented, if not currently available—to help the able-bodied poor begin to assume such responsibilities. For it is in meeting these responsibilities that they experience the vindication of their own dignity as citizens, and not in any other way. We have heretofore thought much too little about finding ways in which the able-bodied poor might, for example, find satisfaction in being of assistance to each other. It is wrong and quite mischievous to think of them as clients merely, as victims, as passive recipients of benefits received from others. As much as anything, they suffer from social disorganization. Structures, therefore, must be developed through which they can learn to help each other. These structures, in turn, should tie them fruitfully into the wider society, as its full and active members. Given favourable circumstances, the poor are the best agents of each other's welfare, not in isolation from the rest of us, but in community with us.

I am trying to draw a contrast here between two different mental constructions concerning how to help the poor. One mental construction projects a large set of clients, now marginalized, to whom goods must be delivered to bring them up to a level of relative equality with others. In the other mental construction, the social task consists of so arranging an abundance of opportunities that the poor can become the agents of their own development, personal and economic, and gain power over an ever broader array of personal decisions in their own lives. One construction focuses on giving to the poor. The other construction focuses on multiplying opportunities among the poor, so that the poor can rise as far as their talents take them. It goes without saying that I believe the second to more humane, more Christian, and more promising than the first.

In this light, public policy designed to stimulate the appropriation of personal responsibility by every citizen without exception—and thus especially to liberate the poor—should be designed to elicit their innate capacities and to bring these to fruition. Social assistance, given generously, ought to operate under the strict criterion of personal liberty; namely, that it generates in all a sense of responsibility, both to their own possibilities and to one another.

7 Conclusion

We are, I believe, at a new threshold of social advancement. Many of the old ways are not working. We need to rethink our aims. We need to rethink our methods. To meet this task, I have proposed for your consideration the third of the conceptions of liberty available in our tradition, but much neglected. The origins of this conception lie in Judaism and Christianity, but its sweep is universal, and its present social possibilities have been enhanced by many secular institutional experiments. This concept obliges us to reconsider the moral content of liberty, both for individuals and for societies. It goes well beyond negative liberty. It also prevents positive liberty from becoming the engine of a new soft despotism.

My final appeal is this: the promise of liberty—political liberty, economic liberty, and moral liberty—must not lie fallow in this generation, favoured as we have been by the fruits of so many sacrifices made by so many in the past. The tradition of liberty is (in Chesterton's phrase) the democracy of the dead, and the social edifice of liberty is not in any generation made complete. There is always more to do. The urgent question of the present time is how to liberate, and not make servile, the able-bodied poor. Whoever answers that question best will have the next age in his debt.

Notes

1 Robert Heilbroner, *The New Yorker*, 23 January 1989, p. 98.

2 Thomas L. Pangle, *The Spirit of Modern Republicanism: The Moral Vision of the American Founders and the Philosophy of Locke*, Chicago: University of Chicago Press, 1988.

3 Raymond Plant, *Citizenship, Rights and Socialism*, Fabian Tract No. 531, London: College Hill Press, 1988, p. 2.

4 Peggy Noonan, *What I Saw at the Revolution: Political Life in the Reagan Era*, New York: Random House, 1989, p. 346.

5 Lester Thurow, 'Who Stays Up With the Sick Cow?', a review of *The Capitalist Revolution*, by Peter L. Berger, *The New York Times Book Review*, 7 September 1986, p. 9.

6 'The social question began to play a revolutionary role only when, in the modern age and not before, men began to doubt that poverty is inherent in the human condition, to doubt that the distinction between the few, who... had succeeded in liberating themselves from the shackles of poverty, and the labouring poverty-stricken multitude was inevitable and eternal. This doubt, or rather the conviction that life on earth might be blessed with abundance instead of being cursed by scarcity, was American in origin; it grew directly out of the American colonial experience.' (Hannah Arendt, *On Revolution*, New York: The Viking Press, 1965, p. 15.)

7 Alexis de Tocqueville, *Democracy in America*, edited by J.P. Mayer and translated by George Lawrence, New York: Anchor Books, 1966, p. 513.

8 'To study the Union before studying the state,' wrote Tocqueville, 'is to follow a path strewn with obstacles. The federal government was the last to take shape in the United States; the political principles on which it was based were spread throughout society before its time, existed independently of it, and only had to be modified to form the republic...
[American] political and administrative life is concentrated in three active centres, which could be compared to the various nervous centres that control the motions of the human body. The township is the first in order, then the county, and last the state.' (*ibid.*, p. 61.)

9 Daniel J. Boorstin, *The Americans*, vol. 1, *The Colonial Experience*, New York: Random, 1958.

10 Nathan Rosenberg and L.E. Birdzell, Jr., *How the West Grew Rich: The Economic Transformation of the Industrial World*, New York: Basic Books, 1986.

11 'Latin Americans and their leaders have not considered that the idea of progress and the desire for innovation have determined the course of recent history. We belong to another tradition, the Hispanic or Hispanic-Roman, which thinks of society as immutable. It has a slow vegetable growth which unfolds in a fixed pattern and relegates creativity to an ornamental level...
We do not realise that in almost five centuries at a university such as San Marcos, hardly a discovery of scientific importance was made, and not one original idea was advanced in the humanities...

[Our poor revolutionaries] do not understand that in these modern times the most profound revolutions take place not in the barracks or in the mountains, but in the laboratories and in the offices of the most daring intelligentsia.' (Carlos Alberto Montaner, *Cuba, Castro and the Caribbean: The Cuban Revolution and the Crisis in Western Conscience*, trans. Nelson Duran, New Brunswick, New Jersey: Transaction Books, 1985, pp. 2-4.)

12 'The great difference,' wrote Abraham Lincoln, between ancient times and his own, 'is the result of Discoveries, Inventions and Improvements. These, in turn, are the result of observation, reflection and experiment.' See his 'Lecture on Discoveries and Inventions' delivered in Jacksonville, Illinois on 11 February 1859. Printed in *Abraham Lincoln: Speeches and Writings 1859-1865*, New York: Library of America, 1989, pp. 3-11.

13 Alexander Hamilton, James Madison, John Jay, *The Federalist Papers*, with an introduction by Clinton Rossiter, New York: New American Library, 1961, No. 10, p. 84.

14 'The protection of these faculties [the diverse faculties of men, from which the rights of property originate] is the first object of government.' (*ibid.*, No. 10, p. 78.) 'Justice is the end of government.' (*ibid.*, No. 51, p. 324.)

15 See Jennifer L. Hochschild, 'Why There is No Socialism in the United States' and 'Political Orientations: Why the Dog Doesn't Bark', chapters 1 and 9, in *What's Fair? American Beliefs About Distributive Justice*, Cambridge, Mass: Harvard University Press, 1981.

16 *Years of Poverty, Years of Plenty: The Changing Economic Fortunes of American Workers & Families*, Greg J. Duncan *et al.*; Institute for Social Research, 1984.

17 See the Roper Report on job satisfaction, No. 88-100, January 1989. Although this report suggests that job satisfaction has declined somewhat since 1973, in 1988 85 per cent of those polled still answered that they were 'extremely satisfied' or 'fairly well satisfied' with their jobs, everything considered.

18 Daniel Bell, *The Cultural Contradictions of Capitalism*, New York: Basic Books, 1976.

19 See Nicholas Phillipson, 'Adam Smith as Civic Moralist', in Istvan Hont and Michael Ignatieff, eds., *Wealth and Virtue: The Shaping of Political Economy in the Scottish Enlightenment*, Cambridge: Cambridge University Press, 1983, pp. 179-202.

20 Thomas Jefferson, *The Life and Selected Writings of Thomas Jefferson*, Adrienne Koch and William Peden, eds., New York: Modern Library, 1972, p. 311.

21 'A special rule [of Divine providence] applies where intelligent creatures are involved. For they excel all others in the perfection of their nature and the dignity of their end: they are masters of their activity and act freely, while others are more acted on than acting.' (Thomas Aquinas, III *Contra Gentiles*, III-16, in *Saint Thomas Aquinas: Philosophical Texts*, selected and translated by Thomas Gilby, New York: Oxford University Press, 1960, pp. 355-6.)

'Men are principals, not merely instruments... Providence directs rational creatures for the welfare and growth of the individual person, not just for the advantage of the race.' (Thomas Aquinas, III *Contra Gentiles*, III-16, in *ibid.*, pp. 356-7.)

22   Alasdair MacIntyre, *After Virtue*, Notre Dame: University of Notre Dame Press, 1981, pp. 6-10.

23   'Ambition,' wrote James Madison, 'must be made to counteract ambition... It may be a reflection on human nature that such devices should be necessary to control the abuses of government. But what is government itself but the greatest of all reflections on human nature? If men were angels, no government would be necessary. If angels were to govern men, neither external nor internal controls on government would be necessary.' (*The Federalist*, No. 51, p. 322.)

24   'It should be noted that in today's world, among other rights, the right of economic initiative is often suppressed. Yet it is a right which is important not only for the individual but also for the common good.' (Pope John Paul II's encyclical, *Sollicitudo Rei Solialis*, Vatican City, 1987, para. 15.)

25   Israel M. Kirzner, *Discovery and the Capitalist Process*, Chicago: The University of Chicago Press, 1985; Michael Novak, 'The Virtue of Enterprise', *Crisis*, May 1989, pp. 19-25.

26   Hernando de Soto, *The Other Path: The Invisible Revolution and the Third World*, foreword by Mario Vargas Llosa, and June Abbott, trans. New York: Harper and Row, 1989.

27   See *Sollicitudo Rei Socialis*, 33, where Pope John Paul sums up his argument with these words: 'In order to be genuine, development must be achieved within the framework of solidarity and freedom, without ever sacrificing either of them under whatever pretext.'

28   'The numbers of people for whom such communitarian visions are good and mean something at the level of their everyday experience are declining, attenuating their moral force... the socialist has to be realistic and recognise the individualism of the age.' (Raymond Plant, Fabian Tract 531, p. 2.)

29   Michael Novak, 'The Return of the Catholic Whig', *First Things*, March 1990, pp. 38-42. See also, 'The Communitarian Individual', chapter VII in *The Spirit of Democratic Capitalism*, New York: Simon & Schuster, 1982, pp. 143-150.

30   M. Weber, *The City*, New York: The Free Press, 1958, chapter 2, 'The Occidental City'; see also F.H. Knight, *The Economic History*, trans., New York: Collier Books, 1966, chapter 28, 'Citizenship', pp. 233-49.

31   F.A. Hayek, *The Collected Works of F.A. Hayek*, ed. Bartley, W.W., III, vol. I, *The Fatal Conceit: The Errors of Socialism*, Chicago: University Chicago Press, 1988, p. 66.

32   Socialism has not died, of course, as an organised partisan position. Nonetheless, in intellectual terms, nearly all the old 'defining differences' have had to be abandoned: the labour theory of value, the abolition of private property, the elimination of markets, the nationalisation of industry, economic trust in rational planning elites, antagonism to incentives and profits, and the one-sided emphasis on distribution (to the neglect of the creation of new wealth and even to long-range ecological investments). Moreover, much too little attention was paid by early socialists to the danger of the 'new class', the one-party state, the diminishment of private ('bourgeois') rights, the grayness of aspect of thoroughly socialist societies, etc. The early socialist faith, for all its admirable energy and 'idealism', was much too utopian, optimistic, and unsophisticated. It was indifferent to the systemic checks and balances on political power that common sense would have recommended. Those who today call themselves socialists have abandoned nearly all the central commitments of

their socialist predecessors, and advance a faith highly refined indeed. There are signs of a more empirical temper; this is all to the good.

33 Raymond Plant, Fabian Tract, 531.

34 Isaiah Berlin, 'Two Concepts of Liberty', *Four Essays on Liberty*, Oxford: Oxford University Press, 1969, pp. 118-72. By 'negative' freedom, Berlin means 'not being interfered with by others. The wider the area of non-interference the wider my freedom' (p. 123). The 'positive' sense of freedom is more complex: it 'derives from the wish on the part of the individual to be his own master. I wish my life and decisions to depend on myself, not on external forces of whatever kind. I wish to be a subject, not an object; to be moved by reasons, by conscious purposes, which are my own, not by causes which affect me, as it were from outside. I wish to be somebody, not nobody; a doer—deciding, not being decided for, self-directed and not acted upon by external nature or by other men as if I were a thing, or an animal, or a slave incapable of playing a human role, that is, of conceiving goals and policies of my own and realizing them... I wish, above all, to be conscious of myself as a thinking, willing, active being, bearing responsibility for my choices and able to explain them by references to my own ideas and purposes' (p. 131). Berlin's main worry about the second form of freedom, 'positive freedom' is that in the hands of rationalists it can lead to despotism. See especially pp. 145-54.

35 The religious notion of liberty, Acton notes, is quite different from the modern secular view (such as in Isaiah Berlin's 'Two Concepts'), and proceeds by 'defining liberty not as the power of doing what we like, but the right of being able to do what we ought.' (Dalberg-Acton, J.E.E., *Essays in Religion, Politics, and Morality: Selected Writings of Lord Acton*, ed., Fears, J.F., vol. III, Indianapolis: Liberty Classics, 1988, p. 613.) Compare with note 39 below.

36 See the sections of 'Liberty' and 'Conscience' in Acton, *ibid.*, pp. 489-508. Note especially the interplay between strictly moral and fully political understandings of 'liberty', and individual and social dimensions of 'conscience'. See also John Gray, 'On Negative and Positive Liberty', *Liberalisms*, London: Routledge, 1989, pp. 45-68. I have been much helped by Gray's essay.

37 T.L. Pangle, 'Locke, Jefferson, and Liberal Education', unpublished lecture delivered at the American Enterprise Institute, 13 February, 1990.

38 Phillipson, 'Adam Smith as Civic Moralist', *op. cit.*

39 Tocqueville, A. de., *Democracy in America*, p. 46, quotes Cotton Mather as follows: 'Nor would I have you mistake in the point of your own liberty. There is a liberty of corrupt nature, which is affected by men and beasts to do what they list; and this liberty is inconsistent with authority, impatient of all restraint... But there is a civil, a moral, a federal liberty, which is the proper end and object of authority; it is a liberty for that only which is just and good...'

40 'Liberty,' Acton wrote, 'has not subsisted outside of Chirstianity. Providence, while it summons a larger part of mankind to the enjoyment of truth, which is the blessing of religion, has called a larger part of mankind to the enjoyment of freedom, which is the blessing of the political order—that freedom should be religious, and that religion should be free.' (Lord Acton, *Essays in Religion, Politics, and Morality*, p. 491.) For Acton's discussion of the historical relation between liberty and the Christian notion of conscience, see *ibid.*, pp. 29-30.

41 'Liberty is the prevention of control by others. This requires self-control and, therefore, religious and spiritual influences: education, knowledge, well-being.
Liberty becomes a question of morals more than of politics.' (*ibid.*, p. 490.)

42 'Liberty depends on the division of power. Democracy tends to unity of power. To keep asunder the agents, one must divide the sources; that is, one must maintain, or create separate administrative bodies. In view of increasing democracy, a restricted federalism is the one possible check upon concentration and centralism.' (*ibid.*, p. 558.)

43 St. Thomas Aquinas, *Summa Theologiae*, Gilby, T., general ed., vol. 35, *The Consequences of Charity*, New York: Blackfriars, 1972, p. 7 (2a2ae, 34, I). See also, vol. 25, *Sin*, especially pp. 23-5.

44 'In framing a government which is to be administered by men over men, the great difficulty lies in this: you must first enable the government to control the governed; and in the next place oblige it to control itself. A dependence on the people is, no doubt, the primary control on the government; but experience has taught mankind the necessity of auxiliary precautions.' (*Federalist*, No. 52, p. 322.) Madison prided himself on his attention to these 'auxilliary precautions', such as discerning carefully the sources of ambition (and counter ambition) in the diverse public offices, even independently of the persons who would occupy them.

45 I have always liked Reinhold Niebuhr's instinct for these things, as expressed, e.g., in *Moral Man and Immoral Society*, New York: Charles Scribner's Sons, 1932, and *The Irony of American History*, Charles Scribner's Sons, 1952.

46 For a rather brilliant treatment of this point, see Bernard Lonergan, *Insight, A Study of Human Understanding*, New York: Philosophical Library, 1958, pp. 666-7.

47 Hayek, F., *The Fatal Conceit*, p. 21. Hayek sums up his argument about the attempt to impose a rational plan on society in a section headed, 'How What Cannot Be Known Cannot Be Planned', *ibid.*, pp. 85-8.

48 *The Federalist*, No. 10, p. 84.

49 See the discussion of subsidiarity in *Toward the Future: Catholic Social Thought and the U.S. Economy*, New York: Lay Commission on Catholic Social Teaching and the U.S. Economy, 1984, pp. 5-6. The concept has been developed by Roger Heckel, S.J., *Self-Reliance*, Vatican City: Pontifical Commission on Justice and Peace, 1978, pp. 21-3. Oswald von Nell-Breuning writes that 'Abraham Lincoln had formulated [the principle of subsidiarity] thus for practical use: "The legitimate object of government is to do for a community of people whatever they need to have done but cannot do at all, or cannot so well do for themselves in their separate and individual capacities. In all that people can individually do as well for themselves, government ought not to interfere."' ('Subsidiarity', in *Sacramentum Mundi: An Encyclopedia of Theology*, 6 vols., New York: Herder and Herder, 1970, VI, p. 115.)

50 Hilaire Belloc, *The Servile State*, Indianapolis: Liberty Classics, 1977.

Other Health and Welfare Unit Publications

Competing for the Disabled

September 1989, £5.00. ISBN 0-255 36256-0

PROFESSOR C. S. B. GALASKO, *Consultant Orthopaedic Surgeon, Manchester*
PROFESSOR IAN McCOLL, *Director of Surgery, Guys Hospital*
CAROLINE LIPKIN, *IEA Health Unit*

'It would be wrong to this IEA publication as simply another broad right-wing sideswipe at state-funded health provision. It offers a level of detail and thoughtfulness which is likely to appeal beyond its normal constituency.'   *Health Service Journal*

If you need a wheelchair you are advised to be rich ... Governments should not, [the authors] conclude, both finance and control the production of health care services, since the disadvantages are borne by the disabled.'   *The Lancet*

Perestroika in the Universities

November 1989, £5.00. ISBN 0-255 36257-9

PROFESSOR ELIE KEDOURIE, *London School of Economics*

'The Government was yesterday accused of seeking to "nationalise" the universities by increasing central control over their activities through the new Universities Funding Council. Professor Kedourie said it was "quite mysterious" that a Conservative administration should follow a university policy "so much at variance with its proclaimed ideals".'   *The Times*

Medical Care: Is it a Consumer Good?

April 1990, £3.95. ISBN 0-255 36258-7

BRENDAN DEVLIN, *Consultant Surgeon, North Tees General Hospital*
IAIN HANHAM, *Consultant Radiotherapist and Oncologist, Westminster Hospital*
JAMES LE FANU, *General Practitioner*
ROBERT LEFEVER, *General Practitioner*
BRIAN MANTELL, *Consultant in Radiotherapy and Oncology, The London Hospital*
MICHAEL FREEMAN, *Consultant Orthopaedic Surgeon, The London Hospital*

'Devlin ... points out that the quality of practice is by no means assured: doctors, he claims, do not always elicit the correct history, and they can overlook or misinterpret physical signs; 30-40% of appendices removed in Britain show no evidence of appendicitis.'   *The Lancet*